ANIMALS
LIFE IN THE FREEZER

PUFFINS

by Ruth Owen

WINDMILL BOOKS

New York

Published in 2013 by Windmill Books, An Imprint of Rosen Publishing
29 East 21st Street, New York, NY 10010

Produced for Windmill by Ruby Tuesday Books Ltd
Editor for Ruby Tuesday Books Ltd: Mark J. Sachner
US Editor: Sara Antill
Designer: Emma Randall
Consultant: Stephen W. Kress, Director, Seabird Restoration Program, National Audubon Society, Ithaca, New York

Photo Credits:
Cover, 1, 7, 8–9, 10–11, 12–13, 14–15, 16–17, 18–19, 21, 22, 25, 27, 28–29 © Shutterstock; 4–5, 24 © Alamy; 7 (bottom right) © Tokumi, Wikipedia Creative Commons; 20, 23 © FLPA.

Publisher Cataloging Data

Owen, Ruth, 1967–
 Puffins / by Ruth Owen.
      p. cm. — (Polar animals—life in the freezer)
  Includes index.
Summary: This book tells about Atlantic puffins including physical characteristics, habitat, feeding habits, and how they raise their young.
Contents: Coming home — The world of the Atlantic puffin — Fantastic feathers, beautiful beaks – In the water, in the air — What's on the menu? — Puffin romance — Building a burrow — A precious egg — Raising a puffling — Life in a colony — Humans and puffins — Dangers to puffins — The future for puffins.
 ISBN 978-1-4777-0224-6 (library binding) — ISBN 978-1-4777-0235-2 (pbk.) — ISBN 978-1-4777-0236-9 (6-pack)
 1. Atlantic puffin—Juvenile literature   [1. Puffins]   1. Title
2013
598.3/3

Manufactured in the United States of America

CPSIA Compliance Information: Batch # BW13WM: For Further Information contact Windmill Books, New York, New York at 1-866-478-0556

COMING HOME

On a cliff top high above an ice-cold ocean, a little black and white bird is very busy.

The bird has been out at sea for many years. Today is the first time he has been on land since he left his parents. Now, he has returned to the place where he hatched from an egg in his parents' underground **burrow** four years ago.

CONTENTS

The bird is an Atlantic puffin and he is busy digging his own burrow on the cliff top. His **mate** is helping him. When the burrow is ready, she will lay an egg in their new home, and the young puffins will become parents themselves!

Atlantic puffins are small seabirds that live in and around the **Arctic Circle**. Their scientific Latin name is *Fratercula arctica*. It means "little brother of the north."

The "little brother" part of the puffin's Latin name may be linked to the use of the word "brother" to mean a monk or friar. This is because the birds' black feathers look a little like a monk's robes and hood.

An Atlantic puffin pair at their cliff top burrow

THE WORLD OF THE ATLANTIC PUFFIN

Atlantic puffins are found in the North Atlantic Ocean. From late summer to spring they live out in the cold ocean. They spend the winter far from land, and very little is known about their lives at sea.

Spending months at a time in the ocean is not a problem for a puffin, however. It has waterproof feathers, eats fish, and unlike most animals, can drink salty seawater if it gets thirsty.

WHERE ATLANTIC PUFFINS LIVE

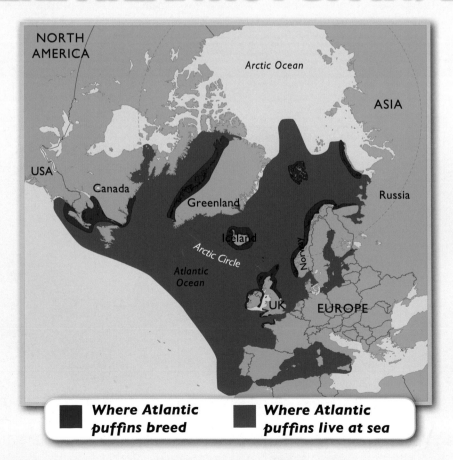

NORTH AMERICA
Arctic Ocean
ASIA
USA
Canada
Greenland
Russia
Iceland
Arctic Circle
Norway
Atlantic Ocean
UK
EUROPE

◼ **Where Atlantic puffins breed**   ◼ **Where Atlantic puffins live at sea**

From April to August, adult puffins come ashore to breed on rocky cliffs. Hundreds or thousands of puffin couples will gather in one area in a **breeding colony.** There are Atlantic puffin breeding colonies on the coastlines of eastern Canada and the northeastern United States, and in Greenland, Iceland, and parts of northern Europe and Russia.

Atlantic puffins swimming in the ocean

There are four types of puffins—Atlantic puffins, horned puffins, tufted puffins, and rhinoceros auklets. Horned and tufted puffins and rhinoceros auklets live in the northern Pacific Ocean, from the east coast of Asia to the west coast of North America.

Horned puffin

Tufted puffin

Rhinoceros Auklet

7

FANTASTIC FEATHERS, BEAUTIFUL BEAKS

A puffin's black back and white belly are a form of **camouflage** to protect it from **predators** when it is at sea.

If seen from above, the bird's black feathers help it blend into the dark ocean. If seen from underwater, its white belly helps it blend with bright sunlight filtering through the water.

A puffin's large orange and grayish-blue beak is its most eye-catching and unusual physical feature. During the summer mating season a puffin's beak becomes more vibrant and colorful. In winter, when the bird is at sea, the colors are duller and the blue sections of the beak fall off.

A puffin's wingspan measures about 24 inches (61 cm) from wing tip to wing tip.

The colorful beaks of Atlantic puffins give them their nickname of "parrots of the sea."

An adult puffin is usually between 10 and 12 inches (25–30 cm) tall. It weighs just over 1 pound (500 g). That is just a little more than a can of soda.

IN THE WATER, IN THE AIR

Puffins are fast flyers and excellent underwater swimmers.

When diving in the ocean to catch fish, puffins use their wings to push themselves through the water. It almost looks as if they are flying underwater. They use their webbed feet to steer and change direction. Puffins can stay underwater for about a minute, but most dives last for around 30 seconds.

In the air, puffins can reach flying speeds of up to 55 miles per hour (89 km/h). They beat their wings very fast—up to seven beats a second. A puffin's wings move so fast that they become a blur!

In years gone by, some people used to say that the puffin was a cross between a bird and a fish because it could swim so well underwater. This allowed people who followed the Catholic religion to eat puffins on Fridays when the eating of meat was forbidden, but it was acceptable to eat fish.

A puffin takes off with its little wings a blur!

Adult puffins catch and eat small fish, such as herring, hake, capelin, and sand eels.

Puffins chase their **prey** underwater, diving to depths of up to 190 feet (58 m). Most prey is caught, however, within 100 feet (30 m) of the ocean's surface.

When catching their own food, puffins swallow their prey immediately. If they are catching fish to feed to their chicks, however, they gather a number of fish in their beaks and then carry them back to their young.

Inside a puffin's beak there are spines. The bird's tongue pushes its catch onto the spines. With the fish safely pinned inside, the bird can then open its beak to catch more.

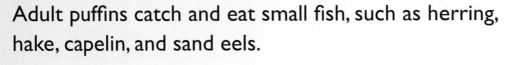

A puffin with a catch
of fish in its beak

A puffin will
usually catch and
carry around 10 fish in
its beak at one time.
A puffin in the United
Kingdom was once
recorded, however,
holding 62 fish
at once!

PUFFIN ROMANCE

Puffins spend the first four to five years of their lives in the open ocean. Once they reach adulthood, they return to the breeding colony where they were born.

Scientists do not know how puffins find their birthplace. One theory is that they create a map in their memory, which they use when it is time to return. The map might use star positions, sounds, smells, or views of the land and ocean to lead the animal home.

Out at sea, the young puffins find partners, and mating takes place in the ocean. Then the birds come ashore along with thousands of other couples.

Puffins are **monogamous**, which means they usually stay with the same mate for their whole lives. Once a puffin pair is together, they will meet up at the breeding colony to mate every year.

A pair of puffins "billing"

Puffin couples sometimes rub their beaks, or bills, together. This shows their **bond** and is known as "billing." Other puffins will sometimes gather around to watch the happy couple and share their excitement!

An Atlantic puffin breeding colony

BUILDING A BURROW

Puffins often build their burrows under rocks on steep, grass-covered cliffs. Building nests in difficult-to-reach places makes it hard for some predators, such as arctic foxes, to take the birds' eggs and chicks.

Male puffins do most of the building work. They use their beaks to dig into and break up the hard soil. Then they shovel away the loosened material with their feet. Puffins dig in the same way that dogs do, throwing the soil out of the burrow hole behind them.

A puffin's burrow is like a tunnel that is dug about 2 to 3 feet (61–91 cm) into the cliff. At the end of the tunnel is the area where the egg will be laid. Here, the puffins make a soft nest of grass and feathers.

Male puffin

Burrow entrance

A puffin holding nesting material in its beak

Once a puffin couple has built a burrow, they may use it year after year.

A PRECIOUS EGG

A female puffin lays just one egg each year. Both parents share the work of caring for their precious egg.

A puffin egg is around 2 inches (5 cm) long. The egg is white and often has brown speckles.

The egg must be kept warm so that the chick inside develops. The male and female puffins take turns doing this important job. They **incubate** the egg by tucking it under one of their wings and then leaning their body against it to keep it warm.

Incubation of the egg lasts for about 42 days. Then the puffin chick inside is ready to hatch!

A life-size photo of an Atlantic puffin egg

Puffins make growling noises. When they are underground in their burrows, the growling noise sounds like a muffled chainsaw.

A puffin pair swaps places in the burrow as they take turns incubating their eggs.

RAISING A PUFFLING

After 42 days a puffin chick, known as a puffling, hatches from the egg inside the burrow. The little puffling has grayish-black and white, fluffy feathers and a grayish-black beak and feet.

The parent birds share the duties of catching food for the chick. Several times a day, each of the parent birds flies out to sea to catch fish. Puffins with chicks usually hunt within about 6 miles (10 km) of the breeding colony. They may travel farther, though, flying up to 50 miles (30 km) from their home to find food.

Puffins usually catch sand eels and fish for their chicks. The parent puffin passes the fish to the chick's beak from its own beak, or it places the fish on the burrow floor for the little puffin to eat.

An Atlantic puffin chick, or puffling

A puffin returns to its burrow from a fishing trip with its beak filled with fish for its chick.

Pufflings make a "peep, peep, peeeeeeep," noise to tell their parents they want food.

LIFE IN A COLONY

Puffin families are in danger from large predatory seabirds.

Great black-backed gulls fly over puffin breeding colonies circling until they spot a lone adult puffin to catch. The large gulls can also catch puffins in mid-air. Herring gulls raid puffin burrows to take their eggs and chicks. Herring gulls may also follow adult puffins as they return to their burrows and then steal the birds' fish.

About six weeks after a puffin chick hatches, it is ready to leave home and go to sea. Now the young bird is called a **fledgling**. Its fluffy feathers have gone and it has sleek black and white feathers.

Puffin Predators

Great black-backed gull

Herring gull

One night, alone and under the cover of darkness, the fledgling leaves its burrow and makes its way to the ocean. Now it will live at sea until it becomes an adult and is ready to find a mate and come ashore at a breeding colony.

Parent puffin

The oldest puffin on record was 36 years old. Scientists have estimated that an average age for a wild puffin is around 20 years.

Puffin fledgling

HUMANS AND PUFFINS

Puffins have been hunted for centuries by some communities in Norway, Iceland, and the Faroe Islands, which are to the north of the United Kingdom.

The Lofoten people of Norway use specially trained dogs to dig the puffins out of their burrows. In Iceland and the Faroe Islands, people use a long pole with a net, called a fleyg, to catch puffins as they fly overhead. These hunters only catch enough puffins to fulfill their communities' needs for meat. They are careful not to damage the puffin populations by killing too many birds.

Fleyg

An Icelandic puffin hunter

Overhunting of puffins has occurred at breeding colonies in other parts of the world, however. Early settlers in Maine overhunted this region's puffin populations for their eggs, meat, and feathers. By 1902, six large breeding colonies had been reduced to just one pair of puffins!

Puffins on a cliff top ledge in the Faroe Islands

Puffins can be badly affected when people overfish an area. In the seas close to a breeding colony on the Norwegian island of Rost, there are no longer enough fish for the adult puffins to catch. This has led to thousands of puffin chicks starving.

DANGERS TO PUFFINS

While most of the time puffins live far from humans, they can still be harmed by manmade **pollution**. **Climate change** may also endanger them in the future.

Sometimes oil is spilled in the ocean from oil drilling operations and oil tankers. Seabirds, such as puffins, can die from swallowing oil. When the birds' feathers become clogged with oil, they are no longer waterproof and cannot protect the birds from freezing ocean waters.

Chemicals from farms and factories often end up in rivers. Then the chemicals flow out into the ocean along with the river water. Puffins may swallow polluted water or be poisoned when they eat fish that have these chemicals inside their bodies.

Puffins were designed by nature to live in cold water and eat coldwater fish. Warmer temperatures caused by climate change may increase ocean temperatures. This could force the puffins' prey fish to move to colder seas that may be far from the birds' breeding colonies.

Warmer temperatures caused by climate change are melting ice in the **Arctic** and in Antarctica. The melting ice could cause sea levels to rise. Some of the small islands where puffins breed could be flooded and disappear forever.

Puffins on the side of a steep cliff

THE FUTURE FOR PUFFINS

Puffins are not **endangered**, but they are now rare in many areas where they once lived. Scientists have been successful, however, in rebuilding a breeding colony that was destroyed by overhunting.

In the 1970s, a program called "Project Puffin" took nearly 1,000 puffin chicks from Newfoundland to Eastern Egg Rock, a small island off the coast of Maine. Scientists became the chicks' parents, bringing them fish everyday. When the chicks went to sea, the scientists had a long wait to find out if their plan would work. It did! When some of the chicks became adults, they returned to Eastern Egg Rock to rear their own chicks and restart a breeding colony.

A puffin breeding colony can be a good thing for its human neighbors because many tourists will want to see the birds. The tourists then spend money in local hotels and shops. It's important, though, that tourists watch the puffins from boats offshore so as not to disturb the busy parent birds.

A scientist holds a fledgling Atlantic puffin

Today, scientists estimate that there are up to 8 million Atlantic puffins living worldwide. To ensure the future survival of Atlantic puffins, breeding colonies must be protected. The ocean water where puffins find their food must also be protected from pollution. Only then will the future be safe for our little brothers of the north.

GLOSSARY

Arctic (ARK-tik)
The northernmost area on Earth, which includes northern parts of Europe, Asia, and North America, the Arctic Ocean, the polar ice cap, and the North Pole.

Arctic Circle
(ARK-tik SIR-kul) One of the major imaginary circles, called circles of latitude, that divide maps and globes of the Earth into different regions. Everything north of the Arctic Circle is called the Arctic.

bond (BOND)
An extremely strong connection.

breeding colony
(BREED-ing KAH-luh-nee)
A large group of animals, made up of males and females, that gather in the same place every year to mate and raise young.

burrow (BUR-oh)
An underground hole or tunnel dug by an animal to use as a permanent home or a temporary place to raise young.

camouflage
(KA-muh-flahj)
Hiding or blending into one's background. An animal's fur or skin color or pattern can camouflage it against its background.

climate change
(KLY-mut CHAYNJ)
The slow warming of planet Earth. Climate change is happening because gases from burning fuels such as coal and oil gather high above the planet and trap the Sun's heat.

endangered (in-DAYN-jerd)
In danger of no longer existing.